FOOTBALL
NUMBER CRUNCH

THIS IS A CARLTON BOOK

Published in 2017 by Carlton Books Limited
an imprint of the Carlton Publishing Group
20 Mortimer Street, London W1T 3JW

Author: Kevin Pettman
Design: RockJaw Creative
Cover design: RockJaw Creative and Kate Wiliwinska
Illustrations: Peter Liddiard, Sudden Impact Media

A catalogue record for this book is available from the British Library.

ISBN: 978-1-78312-284-4

Printed in China

10 9 8 7 6 5 4 3 2 1

FOOTBALL
NUMBER CRUNCH

FIGURES, FACTS AND SOCCER STATS –
THE WORLD OF FOOTBALL IN NUMBERS

KEVIN PETTMAN

CARLTON
KIDS

CONTENTS

PART 1: PLAYERS

Note to readers: the facts and records in this book are accurate to 10 February 2017.

PREMIER LEAGUE: PLAYERS

We kick off *Football Number Crunch* by revealing some amazing numbers and facts about record-breaking Premier League goal kings!

Record Premier League goalscorers

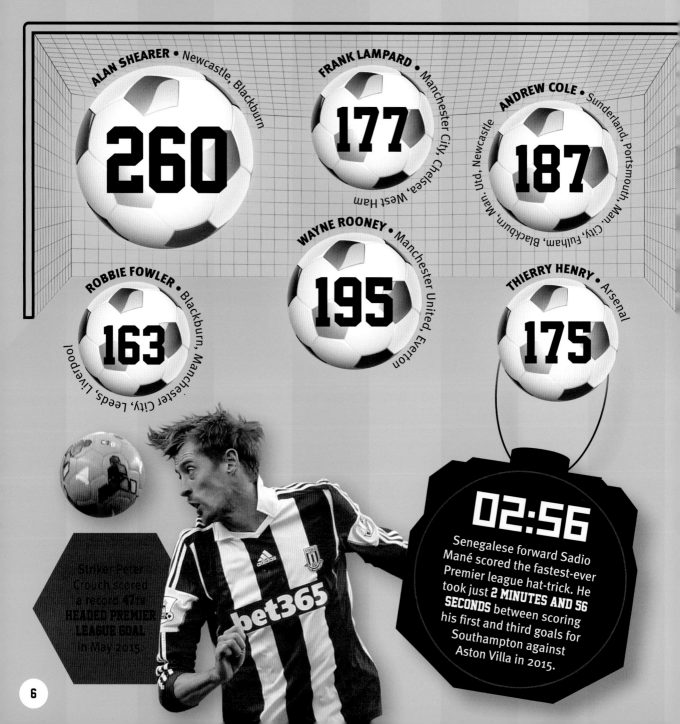

ALAN SHEARER • Newcastle, Blackburn
260

FRANK LAMPARD • Manchester City, Chelsea, West Ham
177

ANDREW COLE • Sunderland, Portsmouth, Man. City, Fulham, Blackburn, Man. Utd, Newcastle
187

WAYNE ROONEY • Manchester United, Everton
195

ROBBIE FOWLER • Blackburn, Manchester City, Leeds, Liverpool
163

THIERRY HENRY • Arsenal
175

Striker Peter Crouch scored a record 47th **HEADED PREMIER LEAGUE GOAL** in May 2015.

02:56
Senegalese forward Sadio Mané scored the fastest-ever Premier league hat-trick. He took just **2 MINUTES AND 56 SECONDS** between scoring his first and third goals for Southampton against Aston Villa in 2015.

6

Craig Bellamy scored for a record **7 DIFFERENT CLUBS** in the Premier League – Coventry, Newcastle, Blackburn, Liverpool, West Ham, Manchester City and Cardiff.

NEWCASTLE UNITED

BLACKBURN ROVERS

LIVERPOOL

MANCHESTER CITY

COVENTRY CITY

CARDIFF CITY

WEST HAM UNITED

Alan Shearer and Andrew Cole have both scored a record **34 PREMIER LEAGUE GOALS** in a single season. Shearer did it in 1994-95 and Cole in 1993-94.

Manchester City's super striker Sergio Agüero scored **5 PREMIER LEAGUE GOALS** against Newcastle in October 2015. Alan Shearer, Andrew Cole, Dimitar Berbatov and Jermaine Defoe have also scored **5 IN ONE GAME**.

In April 2016, Agüero scored his **100TH PREMIER LEAGUE GOAL** for City in just **147 LEAGUE GAMES**.

Leicester striker Jamie Vardy scored in a record **11 PREMIER LEAGUE GAMES IN A ROW** between 29 August and 28 November 2015.

91.9 METRES

91.9 METRES – that's how far goalkeeper Asmir Begovic kicked the ball to score for Stoke against Southampton in 2013. It's the longest goal in Premier League history!

PREMIER LEAGUE: PLAYERS 2

From winner's medals to hitting the woodwork, clean sheets to quickest-ever goals, these players know all about setting Premier League records...

GIGGS

Manchester United legend Ryan Giggs has a stack of Premier League records...

632 The highest number of Premier League appearances.

13 Most Premier League winner's medals.

21 The record number of Premier League seasons that Giggs scored in.

434 Most Premier League wins by a player.

Midfielder Gareth Barry made his Premier League debut in 1998 and by February 2017 had picked up a record **115 YELLOW CARDS**.

Barry has also played over **19,000 PASSES** in his league career.

NUMBER CRUNCH
Striker Robin van Persie hit the post or bar a record **44 TIMES** during his career with Manchester United and Arsenal.

Petr Cech holds the record for the most clean sheets. Between 2004 and February 2017, he kept the ball out of the net in **145 GAMES** for Arsenal and Chelsea.

GOAL!

OWN 10 GOALS

TEAM 11 GOALS

Defender Richard Dunne scored a record **10 OWN GOALS** in the Premier League, just one less than the **11 GOALS** he scored *for* his clubs!

62

That's the highest shirt number ever worn in the Premier League, by Manchester City midfielder Abdul Razak.

Marcus Bent played for a record **8 PREMIER LEAGUE CLUBS** between 1998 and 2011 – Crystal Palace, Blackburn, Ipswich, Leicester, Everton, Charlton, Wigan and Wolves.

WIGAN ATHLETIC

BLACKBURN ROVERS

EVERTON

WOLVERHAMPTON WANDERERS

IPSWICH TOWN

LEICESTER CITY

CHARLTON ATHLETIC

CRYSTAL PALACE

40

Chelsea captain John Terry scored a record **40 PREMIER LEAGUE GOALS** between 1998 and February 2017. No other defender has bagged that many.

GOAL!

10.2 seconds

In 2000, Tottenham defender or midfielder Ledley King scored a goal after **10.2 SECONDS** – the fastest ever in the Premier League.

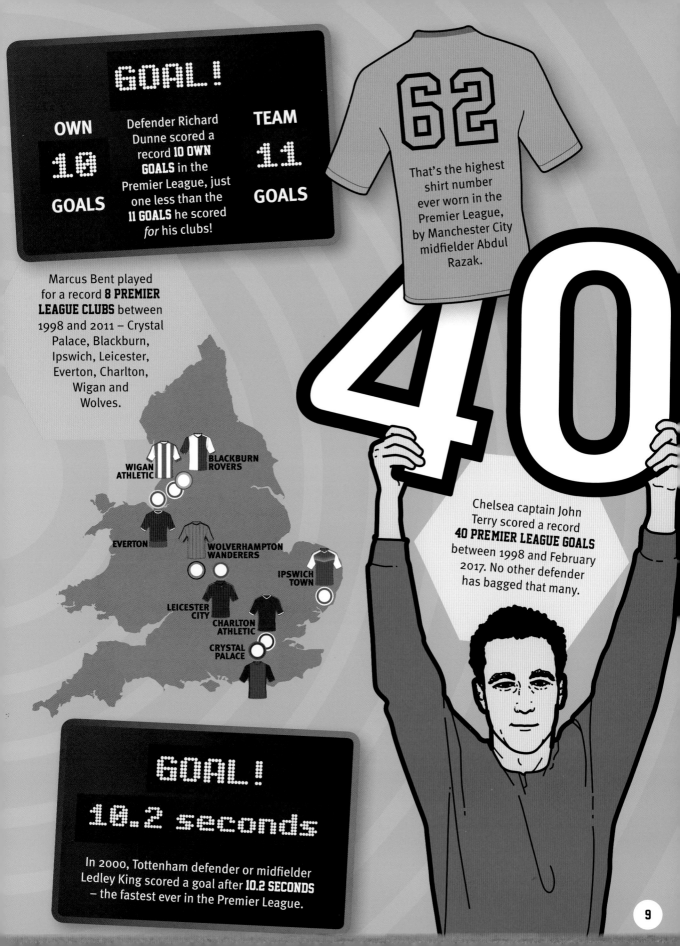

PREMIER LEAGUE: PLAYERS 3

These talented teenagers and youngsters have really ripped up the Premier League record books!

Theo Walcott played for the senior England team when he was 16...

...which was before he'd even made his Premier League debut!

In 2007 Matthew Briggs played for Fulham in the Premier League aged just **16 YEARS AND 65 DAYS**.

Marcus Rashford scored **2 GOALS** on his Premier League debut for Manchester United in 2016, aged just **18**.

£36 MILLION

Manchester United paid Monaco **£36 MILLION** for 19-year-old forward Anthony Martial in 2015 – a Premier League record for a teenager.

4

Between 2012 and 2016, a Tottenham player won **4** of the **5 PFA YOUNG PLAYER OF THE YEAR AWARDS.** Dele Alli, Harry Kane, Gareth Bale and Kyle Walker all took the prize.

When he was **18 YEARS AND 62 DAYS OLD**, striker Michael Owen scored a Premier League hat-trick for Liverpool against Sheffield Wednesday.

The youngest Premier League scorer is James Vaughan (*right*). He was **16 YEARS AND 271 DAYS OLD** when he struck for Everton against Crystal Palace in 2005.

When Chelsea won the title in 2005, the average age of their squad was just **25 YEARS AND 312 DAYS.**

...and Teddy Sheringham is the Premier League's oldest goalscorer – aged **40 YEARS AND 268 DAYS** when he bagged for West Ham against Portsmouth in 2006!

BUNDESLIGA: PLAYERS

Germany's top league has had some top goalscoring heroes over the years...

For Bayern, Müller netted an incredible **533 GOALS** in **585 GAMES** in all competitions.

NUMBER CRUNCH
Bayer Leverkusen winger Julian Brandt scored **6 GOALS** in **6 LEAGUE GAMES IN A ROW** in 2016. He was just **19 YEARS OLD.**

In 1971-72 Müller cracked in **40 BUNDESLIGA GOALS**, the most in a single season.

Gerd Müller struck a record **365 BUNDESLIGA GOALS** in **427 GAMES** between 1965 and 1979.

00:09

Kevin Volland (1899 Hoffenheim) and Karim Bellarabi (Bayer Leverkusen) have both scored a Bundesliga goal just **9 SECONDS** after kick off.

Pierre-Emerick Aubameyang scored an amazing **56 BUNDESLIGA GOALS** in his first **97 GAMES** for Borussia Dortmund.

Mega-fast Aubameyang can sprint **30 METRES** in just **3.8 SECONDS!**

Peru's Claudio Pizarro is the top foreign goalscorer in the Bundesliga with **190 GOALS** from **418 GAMES**.

Top Bundesliga scorers of all time

		Goals	Games
1	Gerd Müller	365	427
2	Klaus Fischer	268	535
3	Jupp Heynckes	220	369
4	Manfred Burgsmüller	213	447
5	**CLAUDIO PIZARRO**	**190**	**418**
6	Ulf Kirsten	182	350
7	Stefan Kuntz	179	449
=8	Klaus Allofs	177	424
=8	Dieter Müller	177	303
10	Hannes Löhr	166	381

Striker Dieter Müller is the only player to have scored **6 BUNDESLIGA GOALS** in one game, for FC Köln in 1977.

LETHAL LEWANDOWSKI

Robert Lewandowski took just **64 GAMES** to score **50 LEAGUE GOALS** for Bayern Munich.

2 x BUNDESLIGA TOP SCORER AWARDS.

First foreign player to score **30 GOALS** in a single season.

74 GOALS in **131 LEAGUE GAMES** for Borussia Dortmund.

09:00

Robert Lewandowski scored **5 GOALS** in just **9 MINUTES** for Bayern in September 2015...

...and he only came into that game as a half-time substitute.

BUNDESLIGA: PLAYERS 2

Here's a stash of award winners, prize takers and record breakers from the Bundesliga.

NUMBER CRUNCH
Nuri Sahin became the youngest Bundesliga player in 2005 after debuting for Borussia Dortmund at **16 YEARS AND 334 DAYS OLD.**

SCHAFF ♥ BREMEN

Manager Thomas Schaff won the Bundesliga with Werder Bremen in **2004.** He was in charge for a huge **14 YEARS.** Schaff also played over **300 GAMES** for the club.

Brazil striker Ailton, who starred for Werder Bremen, was Bundesliga Player of the Year in **2004.** He was the 1st **NON-GERMAN PLAYER** to win it.

Franz Beckenbauer is the only player to win the award **4 TIMES.**

JUPP HEYNCKES

Player
Won **4 BUNDESLIGA TITLES** in the 1970s with Borussia Mönchengladbach.

Manager
Won **3 BUNDESLIGA TITLES** with Bayern Munich in 1989, 1990 and 2013.

82 METRES

£31.4M

Javi Martinez holds the record for the most expensive Bundesliga signing. Bayern Munich bought him from Athletic Bilbao for **£31.4 MILLION** in 2012.

8

Oliver Kahn, Mehmet Scholl and **Bastian Schweinsteiger** have each won a record **8 BUNDESLIGA TITLES.**

82 METRES – that's the longest-distance Bundesliga goal, scored by SC Paderborn's Moritz Stoppelkamp in 2014.

NUMBER CRUNCH
Otto Rehhagel was in charge of a record **832 BUNDESLIGA GAMES** for clubs including Werder Bremen, Borussia Dortmund and Bayern Munich.

BUNDESLIGA: PLAYERS 3

Time to check out these superstar stats all about the most iconic Bundesliga players.

Franz Beckenbauer first won the Bundesliga in **1969** with Bayern. He won **3 MORE TITLES** in the 1970s before winning his **5TH LEAGUE CROWN** in 1982 with Hamburg.

Bayern Munich's Manuel Neuer has kept a record **22 CLEAN SHEETS** in **1 SEASON**. He also let in just **17 GOALS** in a single campaign.

Goalkeeper Harald Schumacher was **42 YEARS OLD** when he won the league with Borussia Dortmund in 1996.

KÖRBEL
602

Karl-Heinz Körbel is the only Bundesliga player to play over 600 games. He made **602 APPEARANCES** for Eintracht Frankfurt.

Bayer Leverkusen star striker Javier Hernandez racked up **17 GOALS** in his first **28 GAMES** after joining the Bundesliga in 2015.

Hamburg defender Manfred Kaltz scored a record 53 **BUNDESLIGA PENALTIES**. He was also an expert crosser – his balls into the box were nicknamed 'banana crosses' because they bent so much!

Pierre-Emerick Aubameyang blasted **3 GOALS** on his Bundesliga debut.

He also scored in **10 LEAGUE GAMES** in a row in 2015.

Bayern Munich legend Thomas Müller scored his first **2 BUNDESLIGA GOALS** after coming on as a substitute in 2009.

Midfield master Kevin de Bruyne made a record **21 ASSISTS** for Wolfsburg in the 2014-15 season.

He's also the most expensive player to leave the Bundesliga after Manchester City bought him for **£47 MILLION**.

LA LIGA: PLAYERS

These La Liga legends have made stacks of epic footy records in Spain's top division.

RONALDO

In his first **7 SEASONS** with Real Madrid, Cristiano Ronaldo scored **30 LA LIGA HAT-TRICKS.**

In 2012 Lionel Messi became the first player to score **50 LA LIGA GOALS** in a season. He scored **84 CLUB GOALS** in total that year!

Fernando Torres was made Atlético Madrid captain when he was just **19 YEARS OLD.**

Diego Maradona scored **45 GOALS** in just **73 GAMES** for Barcelona between 1982 and 1984.

Real Madrid's legendary winger Francisco Gento won a record **12 TITLES** in the 1950s and '60s.

ATHLETIC BILBAO

6

BARCELONA

2

VALENCIA

2

Goalkeeper Andoni Zubizarreta played a record **622 LA LIGA GAMES** for **3 CLUBS.**

QATAR AIRWAYS

NUMBER CRUNCH
Cristiano Ronaldo averages **1.1 GOALS PER GAME** for Real Madrid – a record scoring rate in La Liga.

In 2006 David Villa scored a La Liga hat-trick for Valencia in just **5 MINUTES.**

Luis Suárez is the only player to score **4 LA LIGA GOALS** in consecutive games.

LA LIGA: PLAYERS 2

Study the stats of these superstars of the Spanish game – from talented teenagers to classy keepers.

16 YEARS AND 98 DAYS – that's how old Fabrice Olinga was when he scored for Malaga in 2012. He's the youngest La Liga scorer.

Top 5 players to appear for Barça and Real...

1. Michael Laudrup
2. Ronaldo
3. Bernd Schuster
4. Luis Figo
5. Luis Enrique

Midfielder Michael Laudrup is the only player to win **5 LA LIGA TITLES IN A ROW** with different clubs. He won **4** with Barcelona and a **5TH** with Real Madrid in 1995.

DIEGO'S DIARY '96–'04

IN **2014** DIEGO SIMEONE WAS THE MANAGER OF ATLÉTICO MADRID WHEN THEY WON LA LIGA. **18 YEARS EARLIER**, HE ALSO WON IT AS A PLAYER FOR ATLÉTICO.

X

Barcelona's **3 ATTACKING HEROES** of Messi, Suárez and Neymar have been nicknamed MSN, after the famous website.

Real Madrid's **3 FEARSOME FORWARDS** are known as the BBC – Bale, Benzema and Cristiano.

Barcelona keeper Miguel Reina went **824 MINUTES** without conceding a La Liga goal in 1972-73.

Miguel's son, Pepe, played **30 LA LIGA GAMES** for Barcelona between 2000 and 2002.

NUMBER CRUNCH
Manager Luis Aragones took charge of a mighty **757 LA LIGA GAMES** between 1974 and 2004. He managed **8 CLUBS** in that time.

19

When Sergio Agüero was only **19**, he scored **19 LA LIGA GOALS** for Atlético Madrid in just **1 SEASON**.

In April 2016, Real Madrid's Sergio Ramos was sent off for the **21ST TIME** – a record in La Liga.

LA LIGA
MESSI v RONALDO

They are the two best players on the planet, so check out their numbers and stats in this head-to-head match up...

Statistics accurate to 10 February 2017

	AGE	29
	SHIRT NUMBER	10
	HEIGHT	170cm
	WEIGHT	72kg
	LA LIGA GAMES	366
	LA LIGA GOALS	328
	LA LIGA TITLES	8
	LA LIGA TOP SCORER	3 TIMES
	EUROPEAN GOLDEN SHOE	3 WINS
	CHAMPIONS LEAGUE GAMES	111
	CHAMPIONS LEAGUE GOALS	93
	CHAMPIONS LEAGUE TITLES	4
	INTERNATIONAL GAMES	117
	INTERNATIONAL GOALS	57
	INTERNATIONAL DEBUT	2005
	WORLD PLAYER TITLES	5

HEADED GOALS

LA LIGA	CHAMPIONS LEAGUE
1	0

2015-16 SEASON

GOALS WITH RIGHT FOOT

LA LIGA	CHAMPIONS LEAGUE
2	0

2015-16 SEASON

GOALS WITH LEFT FOOT

LA LIGA	CHAMPIONS LEAGUE
23	5

2015-16 SEASON

NUMBER CRUNCH
Messi was sent off on his Argentina debut. He came on in the 63RD MINUTE but was red carded 2 MINUTES later for a foul!

SEASON 2015-16	GAMES	GOALS	MINUTES PLAYED	ASSISTS	FREE-KICK GOALS	PENALTIES SCORED	PENALTIES WON	SHOTS	FOULS WON
LA LIGA	33	26	2,730	16	4	3	3	155	58
CHAMPIONS LEAGUE	7	6	630	1	0	1	1	39	13

HEADED GOALS

LA LIGA	CHAMPIONS LEAGUE
6	3

2015-16 SEASON

NUMBER CRUNCH
Ronaldo became Real's record goalscorer in October 2015 when he scored his **324TH GOAL** in just **308 GAMES** for the club!

AGE	32
SHIRT NUMBER	7
HEIGHT	185CM
WEIGHT	80KG
LA LIGA GAMES	252
LA LIGA GOALS	274
LA LIGA TITLES	1
LA LIGA TOP SCORER	3 TIMES
EUROPEAN GOLDEN SHOE	4 WINS
CHAMPIONS LEAGUE GAMES	137
CHAMPIONS LEAGUE GOALS	95
CHAMPIONS LEAGUE TITLES	3
INTERNATIONAL GAMES	136
INTERNATIONAL GOALS	68
INTERNATIONAL DEBUT	2003
WORLD PLAYER TITLES	4

GOALS WITH RIGHT FOOT

LA LIGA	CHAMPIONS LEAGUE
20	11

2015-16 SEASON

GOALS WITH LEFT FOOT

LA LIGA	CHAMPIONS LEAGUE
9	2

2015-16 SEASON

SEASON 2015-16	GAMES	GOALS	MINUTES PLAYED	ASSISTS	FREE-KICK GOALS	PENALTIES SCORED	PENALTIES WON	SHOTS	FOULS WON
LA LIGA	36	35	3,183	10	0	6	9	190	38
CHAMPIONS LEAGUE	12	16	1,109	3	0	2	2	66	18

SERIE A: PLAYERS

From Pirlo to Piola and Totti to Trapatonni, feast your eyes on these fab facts from Italy's Serie A.

Giovanni Trapattoni won a record **7 SERIE A TITLES** in total as a manager – **6** with Juventus and **1** with Inter Milan.

RECORD BREAKER

Striker Gonzalo Higuain scored **36 SERIE A GOALS** in 2015-16, equaling the record set by Gino Rossetti in 1929.

NUMBER CRUNCH
Gianluigi Buffon joined Juventus in 2001 for around **£32 MILLION**, which is still a world record for a keeper.

Higuain left Napoli for Juventus in 2016 for **£75.3 MILLION**. That's the highest transfer fee paid in Serie A.

Serie A top scorer Silvio Piola...

- Struck a record **274 SERIE A GOALS** between 1929 and 1954.

- Scored for **5 SERIE A CLUBS.**

- Sadly he won **0 SERIE A TITLES** in his career.

Legendary left-back Paolo Maldini won **7 SERIE A TITLES** with AC Milan between 1988 and 2004. He played a record **648 LEAGUE GAMES** for the club.

On 11 September 2016, Roma hero Francesco Totti scored a record **70TH PENALTY** in the Italian league.

Totti made his Serie A debut **AGED 16** in 1993 and became Roma's club captain at the age of just **19**.

BUFFON

974 MINUTES

Juventus goalie Gianluigi Buffon kept **10 CLEAN SHEETS** in a row in 2015-16. He didn't let in a goal for an amazing **974 MINUTES**.

16

That's the record number of red cards that Juventus defender Paolo Montero picked up in his Serie A career from 1992 to 2005.

10 TOP STARS who have played for rivals AC Milan and Inter Milan: Andrea Pirlo; Roberto Baggio; Christian Vieri; Clarence Seedorf; Mario Balotelli; Zlatan Ibrahimovic; Hernan Crespo; Giuseppe Meazza; Ronaldo; Edgar Davids.

Andrea Pirlo cracked in **28 SERIE A GOALS** from free-kicks. Pirlo starred for AC Milan and Juventus between 2001 and 2015.

SERIE A: PLAYERS 2

Italian football is packed with passion, skill, legends and drama – take in these numbers to become an instant expert.

15

Giuseppe Meazza scored **216 SERIE A GOALS** in **367 GAMES**. He played for fierce rivals Inter Milan and AC Milan in the 1930s and '40s.

The San Siro stadium is also called the Giuseppe Meazza Stadium in honour of him.

Roma's Amedeo Amadei was **15 YEARS AND 280 DAYS OLD** when he debuted in 1937 – the youngest ever Serie A player. Amazingly, Genoa's Pietro Pellegri matched the record in December 2016.

Obafemi Martins would often celebrate scoring for Inter Milan by doing **4 BACKFLIPS** in a row. He scored his first Serie A goal at the age of **18**.

Striker Ivan Zamorano's favourite shirt number was **9**, but he couldn't have it at Inter Milan. So he had 1+8 as his number, because that added up to **9**!

Argentina's Diego Maradona is the most famous Napoli player ever. The awesome attacker led the club to **2 SERIE A TITLES** in 1987 and 1990.

AC Milan's Andriy Shevchenko, Mathieu Flamini and Ronaldinho all had the year they were born as their shirt number!

SHEVCHENKO
76

FLAMINI
84

RONALDINHO
80

Paolo Maldini won **7 TITLES**, but his dad, Cesare, also won **4 SERIE A TROPHIES** at AC Milan. That's **11** between father and son.

Best Juventus players to wear the **NUMBER 10** shirt...

ALESSANDRO DEL PIERO
Michel Platini
Roberto Baggio
Omar Sivori
Carlos Tevez
Giovanni Ferrari
Liam Brady
Paul Pogba
Michael Laudrup

Tough-tackling midfielder Edgar Davids was nicknamed The Pitbull! He won Serie A **3 TIMES** with Juventus.

LIGUE 1: PLAYERS

Fancy finding out about the footy heroes in France's Ligue 1? You'll find everything you need right here.

Marseille forward Josip Skoblar scored a record **44 LIGUE 1 GOALS** in 1970-71.

THE BANK

1 2 - 3 4 - 5 6

Date 16/7/2013

Pay *Striker Edinson Cavani is the most expensive signing in Ligue 1 history. Mega-rich PSG splashed out £55 million to buy him from Napoli.*

£55,000,000·00

Do not mark below this line

⑈1 2 3 4 5⑆ 6 7⑈ 89 1⑈3 1 4

Free-kick king Juninho once scored for Lyon from **37.2 METRES** in Ligue 1.

37.2 METRES

Zlatan Ibrahimovic slammed in a Ligue 1 hat-trick in just **9 MINUTES** for PSG in March 2016.

In total Zlatan scored an incredible **113 LIGUE 1 GOALS** in just **122 GAMES**.

NUMBER CRUNCH
Keeper Mickael Landreau played a record **618 LIGUE 1 GAMES**. His first was for Nantes against Bastia and his last was for Bastia against Nantes!

6 PLAYERS have won Ligue 1 **7 TIMES...**

- Sidney Govou (Lyon)
- Grégory Coupet (Lyon)
- Juninho (Lyon)
- Matthieu Descartes (Lyon)
- Jean-Michel Larque (Saint-Etienne)
- Hervé Revelli (Saint-Etienne)

Speedy winger Kingsley Coman had won **2 LIGUE 1 TITLES** with PSG by the time he was **17**.

2,368 MINUTES

That's how long Anthony Martial played in Ligue 1, with Monaco and Lyon, before his **£36 MILLION** move to Manchester United in 2015. That's the equivalent of fewer than 30 full games!

Jean-Pierre Papin is the only Ligue 1 player to be crowned European Footballer of the Year. He scored **134 GOALS** in **215 GAMES** for Marseille.

Nicolas Anelka joined Arsenal for about **£500,000** from PSG in 1997. Three years later he rejoined PSG for **£20 MILLION**.

£20M

£500K

EUROPEAN LEAGUES: PLAYERS

Countries such as Scotland, the Netherlands, Belgium, Portugal and Turkey all have their own superstar players and super stats from their top-flight leagues.

1982 • 1983 • 1966 • 1967 • 1968 • 1970 • 1972 • 1973

Awesome Ajax forward Johan Cruyff won the Dutch Eredivisie **8 TIMES** in the 1960s, '70s and '80s.

AJAX (1977)

ANDERLECHT (1981)

PORTO (1988)

HAJDUK SPLIT (1974, 1975, 1979)

PANATHINAIKOS (1986)

Legendary Brazil striker Ronaldo played for Dutch side PSV for just one season, but scored **54 GOALS** in **58 GAMES**.

Tomislav Ivic was the first coach to win titles in **5 EUROPEAN LEAGUES**...

- Hajduk Split (then Yugoslavia)
- Ajax (Netherlands)
- Anderlecht (Belgium)
- Panathinaikos (Greece)
- Porto (Portugal)

GOAL! GOAL!

Romelu Lukaku scored **15 GOALS** in 2009-10 to win the Belgian league with Anderlecht, aged only **17**.

Striker Erwin Vandenbergh was top scorer in the Belgian First Division **6 TIMES** in the 1980s and '90s, including **4 IN A ROW**.

12

Cristiano Ronaldo was just **12 YEARS OLD** when he left his home in Madeira to join Sporting Lisbon, in the capital of Portugal.

Hulk is the most expensive signing in the Russian Premier League, costing Zenit St Petersburg **£34 MILLION** in 2012.

242 GOALS in **315 GAMES** – that's the record of Celtic goal machine Henrik Larsson, one of the most feared strikers ever to play in Scotland.

Hakan Sükür is the all-time top scorer in Turkey with **249 SUPER LIG GOALS**.

Grab your calculators, because we reveal even more surprising numbers about top players from leagues all around Europe.

5 BRAZILIANS have won the Primeira Liga Player of the Year award in Portugal, but only **3 PORTUGUESE PLAYERS** have lifted it since it began in 2006.

LEWANDOWSKI

Poland megastar Robert Lewandowski began his career in his home country with Lech Poznan...

82 GAMES
41 GOALS
19 ASSISTS
6,853 MINUTES PLAYED

NUMBER CRUNCH
The Scottish Premier League record transfer is the **£12 MILLION** that Rangers paid for Tore André Flo back in 2000.

Thomas Mavros is a football god in Greece. He scored **260 GOALS** in **501 GAMES** and won the Greek league twice with AEK Athens.

GOAL KING

Manchester United midfielder Henrikh Mkhitaryan once scored **25 GOALS** in **28 GAMES** in **1 SEASON** for Shakhtar Donetsk in Ukraine.

Striker Kenny Miller signed for Rangers **3 TIMES** in his career. He's also one of only a few footballers since 1945 to play for both Rangers and Celtic.

Dutch twins Ronald and Frank de Boer won **5 TITLES** together at Ajax, as well as **1 TITLE** together at Barcelona. Ronald also won **1 TITLE** at Rangers.

Stéphane Chapuisat was top scorer in the Swiss Super League in 2003-04 with **23 GOALS** for Young Boys. He was an 'old boy' though, aged nearly **35**!

Gunnar Nordahl is the only player to be top scorer in Sweden's Allsvenskan league **4 TIMES**. He was also Serie A top scorer **5 TIMES** for AC Milan in the 1950s.

CHAMPIONS LEAGUE: PLAYERS

It's the biggest club competition in Europe and these are some of the biggest stars to set records in the competition.

In 2002-03, Manchester United's Ruud van Nistelrooy set a record by scoring in **9 CHAMPIONS LEAGUE GAMES IN A ROW.**

He struck **56 CHAMPIONS LEAGUE GOALS** in total.

In 2016, Bayern Munich captain Philipp Lahm became the first outfield player to reach **100 CHAMPIONS LEAGUE GAMES** without scoring.

REAL MADRID

90:88

EINTRACHT FRANKFURT

7

3

Real Madrid greats Alfredo Di Stefano and Ferenc Puskás scored **7 GOALS** in the 1960 European Cup final. That's what the Champions League was called before 1992.

Di Stefano is the only player to score in **5 FINALS IN A ROW** (1956–60).

DI STEFANO
27', 30', 73'

PUSKÁS
45+1', 56' (pen), 60', 71'

KRESS
18'

STEIN
72', 75'

German keeper Hans-Jörg Butt scored **3 CHAMPIONS LEAGUE GOALS** between 2000 and 2009.

Arsenal keeper Jens Lehmann was sent off in the **18TH MINUTE** of the 2006 Champions League final. He was the **1ST PLAYER TO BE RED CARDED** in a CL final.

Youngest Champions League-winning coach: Pep Guardiola – **38 YEARS AND 129 DAYS** (with Barcelona in 2009)

Oldest Champions League winning coach: Raymond Goethals – **71 YEARS AND 232 DAYS** (with Marseille in 1993)

Clarence Seedorf is the only payer to win the Champions League with **3 CLUBS** – Ajax (1995), Real Madrid (1998) and AC Milan (2003, 2007).

Xavi Hernandez and Iker Casillas are the only players to make more than **150 CHAMPIONS LEAGUE APPEARANCES.**

As of 10 February 2017, Cristiano Ronaldo had scored **95 CHAMPIONS LEAGUE GOALS** and Lionel Messi had hit **93**.

CHAMPIONS LEAGUE:
PLAYERS 2

Take a look at these awesome Champions League numbers, then impress your mates with your Champions League knowledge.

Zlatan Ibrahimovic has scored Champions League goals for **6 CLUBS** – Ajax, Juventus, Inter Milan, Barcelona, AC Milan and PSG.

18

Club Brugge striker Daniel Amokachi scored the **1ST EVER CHAMPIONS LEAGUE GOAL** in 1992.

Ajax team-mates Patrick Kluivert and Nwankwo Kanu won the Champions League **AGED 18** in 1995. They are the youngest winners of the trophy.

GOAL!

10.12 seconds

That's the quickest goal in Champions League history, scored by Roy Makaay for Bayern Munich in 2007.

62CM

0.5KG

1KG 1KG 1KG

1KG 1KG 1KG 1KG

The Champions League trophy is **62CM TALL** and weighs **7.5KG**.

MESSI'S CHAMPIONS LEAGUE HAT-TRICKS

Arsenal *April 2010*

Viktoria Plzen *November 2011*

Bayer Leverkusen *March 2012*

Ajax *September 2013*

APOEL *November 2014*

Celtic *September 2016*

Manchester City *October 2016*

Lionel Messi has scored a record **7 CHAMPIONS LEAGUE HAT-TRICKS.**

Defender Patrice Evra has lost **4 CHAMPIONS LEAGUE FINALS** – in 2004, 2009, 2011 and 2015.

Ryan Giggs scored in a record **16 CHAMPIONS LEAGUE SEASONS.**

The 2014 Champions League final, between Real Madrid and Atlético Madrid, was watched by a global TV audience of approximately **380 MILLION.**

Roma's Francesco Totti is the oldest scorer of the Champions League era. He was **38 YEARS AND 59 DAYS OLD** when he struck in 2014.

BEST TEAM IN THE WORLD...

Football Number Crunch has smashed all the stats and facts to bring you the best team on the planet. This XI is simply out of this world!

MANUEL NEUER
Neuer won the World Cup in 2014. In total he has played **13 WORLD CUP GAMES**, winning **10** and letting in just **6 GOALS**.

PHILIPP LAHM
Lahm is so good he could play left-back, right-back or midfield in this team. In 2015-16 he scored his **13TH BUNDESLIGA GOAL** in over **350 GAMES**.

DIEGO GODIN
The tough-tackling defender helped Atlético concede just **16 LA LIGA GOALS** in 2015-16 – that's almost half the goals that rivals Real Madrid let in.

SERGIO RAMOS
Ramos scored his **9TH CHAMPIONS LEAGUE GOAL** in the 2016 final against Atlético Madrid to help Real win the trophy for the **11TH TIME**.

DANI ALVES
The rampaging right-back wears number 23 for Juventus, but he also won **23 MAJOR TROPHIES** playing for Barcelona from 2008 to 2016.

SUBSTITUTES:
Neymar (Barcelona & Brazil), Sergio Agüero (Manchester City & Argentina), David De Gea (Manchester United & Spain), Leonardo Bonucci (Juventus & Italy), Robert Lewandowski (Bayern Munich & Poland)

PHILIPP LAHM Bayern Munich & Germany

LB

DIEGO GODIN Atlético Madrid & Uruguay

CD

MANUEL NEUER Bayern Munich & Germany

GK

SERGIO RAMOS Real Madrid & Spain

CD

DANI ALVES Juventus & Brazil

RB

Gareth Bale scored on his **1st CHAMPIONS LEAGUE START** for Real Madrid, against Juventus in 2013.

GARETH BALE Real Madrid & Wales

LM

CRISTIANO RONALDO Real Madrid & Portugal

ST

PAUL POGBA Manchester United & France

CM

LUIS SUÁREZ Barcelona & Uruguay

ST

LIONEL MESSI Barcelona & Argentina

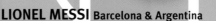

ST

KEVIN DE BRUYNE Manchester City & Belgium

RM

GARETH BALE
Bale scored an amazing **19 LA LIGA GOALS** in just **23 GAMES** in 2015-16. He scored more headers (**9**) than he did with his lethal left foot (**8**).

PAUL POGBA
Pogba won his **4TH SERIE A TITLE IN A ROW** with Juventus in 2016. He won the league every season he played for the Italians.

KEVIN DE BRUYNE
In the 2015-16 season De Bruyne made **15 ASSISTS** and scored **16 GOALS** for Manchester City.

CRISTIANO RONALDO
Ronaldo set two records at EURO 2016. He played in his **21ST EURO FINALS GAME** and scored a record-equaling **9TH TOURNAMENT GOAL**.

LUIS SUÁREZ
In 2016 Suárez scooped the Pichichi Trophy, which is given to La Liga's top scorer, after bagging **40 LEAGUE GOALS** for Barcelona.

LIONEL MESSI
In June 2016 Messi scored his **55TH GOAL** for Argentina in **112 GAMES** to become the country's all-time top scorer.

PREMIER LEAGUE: CLUBS

This stat-packed section reveals fascinating facts from the biggest clubs in the world. We start with England's Premier League, which was created in 1992.

Manchester United are the most successful Premier League club...

13 PREMIER LEAGUE TITLES

Twice won **3 TITLES IN A ROW** (1999, 2000, 2001 and 2007, 2008, 2009)

Manchester United **9-0** Ipswich Town – biggest Premier League home win (1995)

Nottingham Forest **1-8** Manchester United – biggest Premier League away win (1999)

76,098 – highest Premier League attendance, Manchester United v Blackburn (2007)

18 POINTS – biggest Premier League winning points margin (1999-2000)

Between 1992 and 2013, Alex Ferguson won **13 TITLES** and **11 MANAGER OF THE SEASON AWARDS** as manager of Manchester United.

At United, Ferguson won **410 PREMIER LEAGUE GAMES** and collected a record **1,752 POINTS**.

Chelsea's record Premier League scorer is Frank Lampard with **171 GOALS.**

Top 5 Chelsea records

Chelsea reached a record **95 LEAGUE POINTS** in 2004-05.

They scored a record **103 GOALS** in the 2009-10 season.

29 PREMIER LEAGUE GAMES WON in both 2004-05 and 2005-06.

Chelsea are the only team to lose **0 HOME GAMES** in **5 PREM SEASONS.**

In 2004-05 Chelsea let in just **15 PREMIER LEAGUE GOALS.**

ARSENAL 49

Between May 2003 and October 2004 Arsenal went an amazing **49 PREMIER LEAGUE GAMES** without losing.

These clubs haven't been quite so successful in the Premier League...

1	Fewest Premier League wins in a season (Derby County 2007-08)
29	Most defeats in a season (Ipswich Town 1994-95, Sunderland 2005-06, Derby County 2007-08)
14	Sunderland have twice lost 14 home games in a season (2002-03, 2005-06)
20	Fewest Premier League goals scored in a season (Derby County 2007-08)
100	Most Premier League goals conceded in a season (Swindon Town 1993-94)
11	Fewest Premier League points won in a season (Derby County 2007-08)

1992–2016

Just **6 PREMIER LEAGUE CLUBS** HAVE PLAYED IN EVERY PREMIER LEAGUE SEASON – ARSENAL, CHELSEA, EVERTON, LIVERPOOL, MANCHESTER UNITED AND TOTTENHAM.

4 CLUBS HAVE BEEN PROMOTED TO THE PREMIER LEAGUE **4 TIMES** – CRYSTAL PALACE, SUNDERLAND, LEICESTER CITY AND WEST BROMWICH ALBION.

Since winning promotion to the Premier League in 2007, Sunderland have had **9 PERMANENT MANAGERS.**

PREMIER LEAGUE:
CLUBS 2

From managers and money to red cards and record goals, don't miss this crazy collection of Premier League numbers.

The 2011-12 Premier League title race was the closest ever. Manchester City and Manchester United both had **89 POINTS**, but City won the title with a **+64 GOAL DIFFERENCE**.

Chelsea finished the 2009-10 season with a record **+71 GOAL DIFFERENCE**, scoring **103 GOALS** and conceding only **32**.

NUMBER CRUNCH
Liverpool paid Tottenham **£19 MILLION** for Robbie Keane in July 2008, but sold him back to Tottenham for just **£12 MILLION** six months later.

Norwich, Blackburn, Derby County and Birmingham have all kept just **3 CLEAN SHEETS** in a single Premier League season.

The highest-scoring Premier League game is Portsmouth's **7-4 WIN** over Reading in 2007. That's **11 GOALS** conceded!

The highest-scoring draw is the **5-5** game between West Bromwich Albion and Manchester United in 2013.

Keeper Brad Friedel did not miss a Premier League game for **310 MATCHES IN A ROW** for Blackburn, Aston Villa and Tottenham between 2004 and 2012.

Between 1992-93 and 2015-16 Everton were given **84 RED CARDS,** which is more than any other Premier League team.

Tottenham picked up **9 YELLOW CARDS** in their 2-2 draw with Chelsea in May 2016. No other team has collected as many in one game.

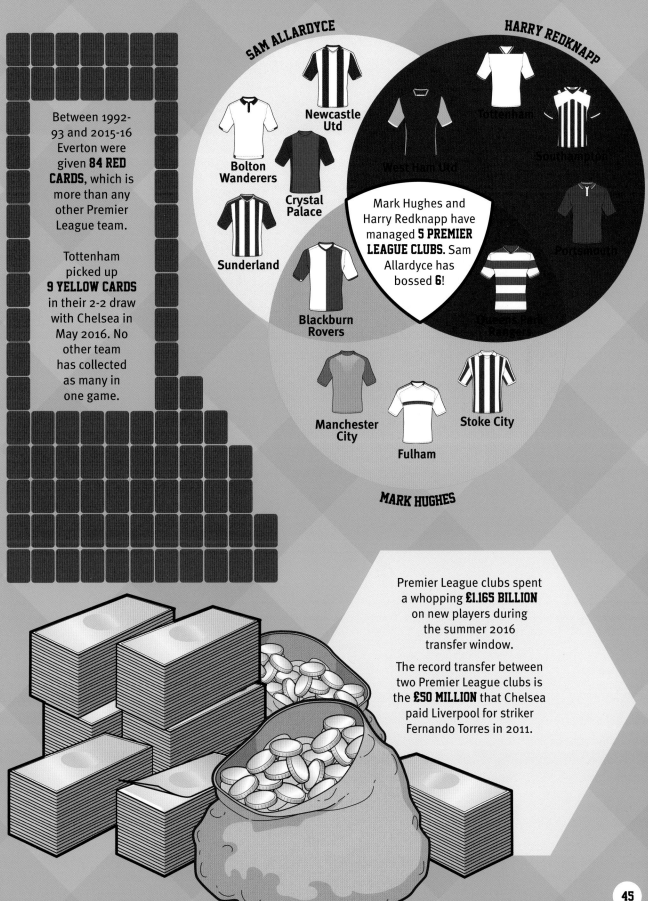

SAM ALLARDYCE

Newcastle Utd

Bolton Wanderers

Crystal Palace

Sunderland

Blackburn Rovers

HARRY REDKNAPP

Tottenham

Southampton

West Ham Utd

Portsmouth

Queens Park Rangers

Manchester City

Fulham

Stoke City

MARK HUGHES

Mark Hughes and Harry Redknapp have managed **5 PREMIER LEAGUE CLUBS.** Sam Allardyce has bossed **6!**

Premier League clubs spent a whopping **£1.165 BILLION** on new players during the summer 2016 transfer window.

The record transfer between two Premier League clubs is the **£50 MILLION** that Chelsea paid Liverpool for striker Fernando Torres in 2011.

PREMIER LEAGUE:
CLUBS 3

Football Number Crunch reveals the biggest footy shocks and surprises ever to hit the Premier League.

In 2009, Sunderland beat Liverpool **1-0** after Darren Bent scored a goal that was deflected into the net by an inflatable beach ball thrown onto the pitch. Bizarre!

In the 1997-98 Premier League season **3 GAMES** were abandoned because the floodlights failed.

Wimbledon were involved in **2** of the games.

90:00

Arsenal suffered a shock **8-2 DEFEAT** at Manchester United in 2011. That's the Gunners' biggest ever loss in the Premier League.

8

WELBECK 21'
YOUNG 29', 90+2'
ROONEY 41', 64', 81' (pen)
NANI 67'
PARK 70'

2

WALCOTT 45+3'
VAN PERSIE 74'

In 2015-16 Leicester City were the shock Premier League champions. They won **81 POINTS**, which was **10 MORE** than second-placed Arsenal.

96:00

In 1993, centre-back Steve Bruce scored in the **86TH** and **96TH MINUTES** as Manchester United miraculously beat Sheffield Wednesday 2-1. The win set up United's **1ST PREMIER LEAGUE TITLE.**

In the 2004-05 season, West Bromwich Albion made history by becoming the **1ST PREMIER LEAGUE CLUB** to escape relegation after being **20TH** on Christmas Day.

The lowest ever Premier League attendance was when a crowd of just **3,039** watched Wimbledon play Everton at Selhurst Park in 1993.

Newcastle had **3 PLAYERS** sent off in a 3-0 defeat to Aston Villa in 2005 – team-mates Kieron Dyer and Lee Bowyer saw red for fighting each other.

Manchester City shocked the Premier League by signing Carlos Tevez from rivals Manchester United in 2009 for about **£47 MILLION**. Tevez won the league and FA Cup with City.

BUNDESLIGA: TEAMS

Here are some fascinating facts about the awesome German league, which was first won in 1964 by FC Köln.

Number of Bundesliga titles

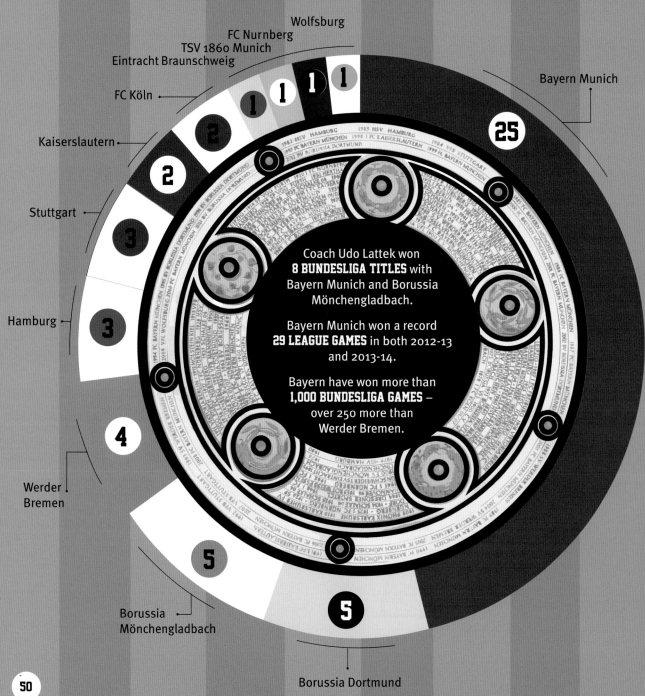

Wolfsburg — 1
FC Nurnberg — 1
TSV 1860 Munich — 1
Eintracht Braunschweig — 1
FC Köln — 2
Kaiserslautern — 2
Stuttgart — 3
Hamburg — 3
Werder Bremen — 4
Borussia Mönchengladbach — 5
Borussia Dortmund — 5
Bayern Munich — 25

Coach Udo Lattek won **8 BUNDESLIGA TITLES** with Bayern Munich and Borussia Mönchengladbach.

Bayern Munich won a record **29 LEAGUE GAMES** in both 2012-13 and 2013-14.

Bayern have won more than **1,000 BUNDESLIGA GAMES** – over 250 more than Werder Bremen.

Borussia Dortmund's Westfalenstadion has the biggest capacity in the Bundesliga. It can hold **81,359 FANS**.

The smallest ground in the 2016-17 Bundesliga season was FC Ingolstadt's Audi Sportpark, with a **15,800 CAPACITY**.

81,359

The **1st TIME** two Bundesliga teams played in the Champions League final was in 2013. Bayern Munich beat Borussia Dortmund **2-1**.

NUMBER CRUNCH
The record Bundesliga attendance was in 1969, when **88,075 FANS** watched Hertha BSC play FC Köln.

Kaiserslautern took just **1 SEASON** to win the Bundesliga after being promoted in 1997, but...

...didn't finish in the **TOP 2** in any of their next **14 BUNDESLIGA CAMPAIGNS**.

The longest unbeaten run in the Bundesliga is **53 GAMES**, set by Bayern between November 2012 and March 2014.

BUNDESLIGA: TEAMS 2

Time to crunch the numbers from some of the Bundesliga's most memorable matches.

12 GOAL! 8

12-0 is the biggest winning margin in the Bundesliga, set in 1978 when Borussia Mönchengladbach thrashed Borussia Dortmund.

The **306 BUNDESLIGA GAMES** in the 1983-84 season produced a record-breaking **1,097 GOALS**.

The lowest number of goals **(790)** were scored in the 1989-90 season.

8 GOAL! 9

The biggest away win was in 1966, when MSV Duisburg beat Tasmania Berlin **9-0**.

A record **4 PENALTIES** were scored in the Borussia Mönchengladbach v Borussia Dortmund league game in 1965.

The dirtiest Bundesliga game was in April 2001 when **13 CARDS** were shown in the Borussia Dortmund v Bayern Munich contest.

NUMBER CRUNCH
On 25 March 2014 Bayern Munich won the Bundesliga title with a record **7 LEAGUE GAMES** still left to play!

HAMBURG
1963

Hamburg are the only German team to have played in every Bundesliga season. Their first league game was in **1963**.

1000

Bayern bashed FC Köln 4-0 in October 2015 to record their **1,000TH BUNDESLIGA VICTORY.**

On 7 May 2016, Bayern Munich won their **4TH BUNDESLIGA TITLE** in a row. No other club has won four consecutive titles.

A record **3 OWN GOALS** were scored when Borussia Mönchengladbach beat Hannover **5-3** in 2009. Hannover scored all **3**.

Allianz Arena

Bayern Munich's **1ST BUNDESLIGA GAME** at their new Allianz Arena stadium was a **3-0 WIN** over Borussia Mönchengladbach in 2005.

They had already defeated the German national team **4-2** at the stadium on 31 May.

LA LIGA: TEAMS

Real Madrid and Barcelona are two of the most famous clubs in the world, and many other top-class teams compete in Spain's entertaining La Liga.

Real Madrid are the only club to have won La Liga **5 TIMES IN A ROW**. They have done this twice.

Barcelona have done the Double (won La Liga and the Spanish Cup in the same season) a record **6 TIMES**.

Real Madrid (2012) and Barcelona (2013) have both picked up **100 LEAGUE POINTS**.

DEPORTIVO
1
TITLE
2000

DEPORTIVO LA CORUNA

ATHLETIC BILBAO

REAL SOCIEDAD

ATHLETIC BILBAO
8 TITLES
1984 1983 1956 1943 1936 1934 1931 1930

REAL SOCIEDAD
2
TITLES
1982 1981

BARCELONA

REAL MADRID

ATLÉTICO MADRID

ATLÉTICO MADRID
10 TITLES
2014 1996 1977 1973 1970 1966 1951 1950 1941 1940

VALENCIA

SEVILLA

REAL BETIS

VALENCIA
6 TITLES
2004 2002 1971 1947 1944 1942

SEVILLA
1
TITLE
1946

REAL BETIS
1
TITLE
1935

REAL MADRID
32 TITLES
2012 2008 2007 2003 2001 1997 1995 1990
1989 1988 1987 1986 1980 1979 1978 1976
1975 1972 1969 1968 1967 1965 1964 1963
1962 1961 1958 1957 1955 1954 1933 1932

BARCELONA
24 TITLES
2016 2015 2013 2011 2010 2009 2006 2005
1999 1998 1994 1993 1992 1991 1985 1974
1960 1959 1953 1952 1949 1948 1945 1929

LOSERS

Sporting Gijon, Logrones, Celta Vigo and Real Betis have all won just **2 GAMES** during a La Liga season.

Athletic Bilbao, Barcelona and Real Madrid have played in every La Liga season since the first in **1929**.

Las Palmas are based in the Canary Islands and have to fly over **2,000KM** to reach Barcelona to play a game.

Eibar's Ipurua Municipal Stadium holds just **6,300 FANS**. That's over **90,000 LESS** than the Nou Camp.

Barcelona and Real Madrid have both scored over **5,000** La Liga goals.

La Liga nicknames

Club	
Malaga	Los Boquerones (The Anchovies)
Espanyol	Periquitos (Budgerigars)
Valencia	Los Murcielagos (The Bats)
Villarreal	El Submarino Amarillo (The Yellow Submarine)

LA LIGA: TEAMS 2

Discover more memorable records involving La Liga's biggest clubs, plus a fab fact about tiny top-flight team Eibar...

In 2016 Real Madrid won a record-equaling **16 LA LIGA GAMES** in a row, scoring **51 GOALS** and conceding only **12** in that run.

3-1   7-1   2-1   4-0   2-1   4-0   5-1   3-0

By 2016 Espanyol had lost over **1,000 LA LIGA GAMES.**

In 2014 the tiny club Eibar played their **1st EVER LA LIGA GAME**. They beat Real Sociedad **1-0.**

Top 5 La Liga local rivalries

1. Real Madrid v Atlético Madrid
2. Sevilla v Real Betis
3. Barcelona v Espanyol
4. Valencia v Villarreal
5. Celta Vigo v Deportivo

RONALDO V RONALDO
Brazil striker Ronaldo, who played for Real Madrid between 2002 and 2006, and Cristiano Ronaldo have both scored against **19 LA LIGA TEAMS** in one season.

3-2   **1-0**   **3-2**   **2-0**   **3-0**   **2-1**   **5-2**   **2-0**

In 2016 Atlético Madrid celebrated the **50TH ANNIVERSARY** of their Vicente Calderon Stadium. Their kit had **3 RED STRIPES** on the front, just like it did in 1966.

Raúl has made the most La Liga appearances for one club. He played **550 GAMES** and scored **228 GOALS** for Real Madrid between 1994 and 2010.

SERIE A: TEAMS

The clubs in Italy's Serie A are some of the world's greatest. Take a look at their awesome achievements.

AC MILAN
18 TITLES
2011 2004 1999 1996 1994 1993 1992 1988 1979
1968 1962 1959 1957 1955 1951 1907 1906 1901

PRO VERCELLI
7 TITLES
1922 1921 1913 1912 1911 1909 1908

INTER MILAN
18 TITLES
2010 2009 2008 2007 2006 1989 1980 1971 1966
1965 1963 1954 1953 1940 1938 1930 1920 1910

GENOA
9 TITLES
1924 1923 1915 1904 1903 1902 1900 1899 1898

BOLOGNA
7 TITLES
1964 1941 1939 1937 1936 1929 1925

TORINO
7 TITLES
1976 1949 1948 1947 1946 1943 1928

ROMA
3 TITLES
2001 1983 1942

JUVENTUS
32 TITLES
2016 2015 2014 2013 2012 2003 2002 1998 1997 1995 1986
1984 1982 1981 1978 1977 1975 1973 1972 1967 1961 1960
1958 1952 1950 1935 1934 1933 1932 1931 1926 1905

2 TITLES
- **FIORENTINA** 1969, 1956
- **NAPOLI** 1990, 1987
- **LAZIO** 2000, 1974

1 TITLE
- **CASALE** 1914
- **NOVESE** 1922
- **HELLAS VERONA** 1985
- **SAMPDORIA** 1981
- **CAGLIARI** 1970

Map labels: PRO VERCELLI, AC MILAN, INTER MILAN, JUVENTUS, CASALE, TORINO, NOVESE, HELLAS VERONA, BOLOGNA, GENOA, SAMPDORIA, FIORENTINA, ROMA, LAZIO, NAPOLI, CAGLIARI

Including the 2016-17 season, Inter Milan have spent a record **85 SEASONS** in the top flight of Italian football.

Inter won a record **17 SERIE A GAMES IN A ROW** between October 2006 and February 2007.

4-1 4-3 2-0 2-1 1-0 2-1 2-0 3-0 2-0

2-0 2-1 3-1 3-1 2-0 2-0 1-0 5-2

AC Milan were the **1st SERIE A CLUB** to win the European Cup, in 1963. They have won it **7 TIMES** in total.

NUMBER CRUNCH
Roma recorded **10 STRAIGHT WINS** at the start of the 2013-14 season. They didn't lose a Serie A game until January 2014.

Home sweet home...

Juventus opened their new **41,000-CAPACITY STADIUM** in 2011 and that season won their first title in **9 YEARS**.

On 5 February 2017 they set a new Serie A record with their **29TH HOME WIN IN A ROW**.

SERIE A: TEAMS 2

Ever wondered why Juve have 3 stars on their kit? Or just how good AC Milan were in the 1990s? Now you'll find out the answers!

AC Milan ruled Italy and Europe from 1988 to 1994, winning **4 SERIE A CHAMPIONSHIPS** and **3 EUROPEAN CUPS/ CHAMPIONS LEAGUES.**

Milan also went an amazing **58 SERIE A GAMES** without losing between May 1991 and March 1993.

NUMBER CRUNCH
In the **1947-48** season, Serie A had **21 CLUBS** in it – so one team always had to sit out a round of games when the others were playing.

Juventus have **3 STARS** on their kit, just above the club badge. Each star represents **10 SERIE A TRIUMPHS.** Juve officially won their **30TH TITLE** in 2014.

x3

Michel Platini

Zinedine Zidane

Pavel Nedved

Omar Sivori

Roberto Baggio

Paulo Rossi

Players with Serie A giants AC Milan and Juventus have won a total of **16 EUROPEAN PLAYER OF THE YEAR AWARDS.** Michel Platini, Marco van Basten and Kaka are some of the winners.

Kaka

x3

Marco van Basten

Gianni Rivera

Andriy Shevchenko

Ruud Gullit

George Weah

Cagliari fly or take a boat trip for all their away Serie A games. They are based on the island of Sardinia and their nearest neighbouring club, Palermo, is about **800KM** away.

In **1907** Palermo changed their red and blue kit to the famous pink and black kit. It was a very unusual colour combination at the time.

The largest Serie A stadium is Inter and AC Milan's San Siro, which holds **80,000 FANS.**

In 2016-17 the smallest ground was Crotone's Stadio Ezio Scida, with a capacity of **9,500.**

Crotone played in Serie A for the first time in 2016, but they won just **1 POINT** from their first **9 GAMES.**

LIGUE 1: TEAMS

It's time to say 'bonjour' to all the biggest, best and record-breaking clubs in the French league.

NUMBER CRUNCH
Monaco's greatest-ever striker is Delio Onnis. He scored **157 LIGUE 1 GOALS** for the club and **299 IN TOTAL** in the league.

2003 • 2004 • 2005 • 2006 • 2007 • 2008 • 2002

7

Lyon won Ligue 1 for a record **7 SEASONS IN A ROW** from 2002 to 2008.

1933
Olympique Lillois won the **1st LIGUE 1 TITLE** in 1933. It was their only triumph before merging with SC Fives to form Lille in 1944.

PSG'S RECORD-BREAKING 2015-16 SEASON...

- **96 LIGUE 1 POINTS** ☑
- **30 WINS** IN THE SEASON ☑
- ONLY **19 GOALS** CONCEDED ☑
- **+83 GOAL DIFFERENCE** ☑

Auxerre's legendary coach Guy Roux took charge of a huge **894 LIGUE 1 GAMES** between 1961 and 2007.

Paris Saint-Germain have dominated Ligue 1 since 2012, but they didn't win their first title until **1986**.

By 1986 Saint-Etienne had already won a record **10 TITLES**!

Lille's **2-0 WIN** over Lyon in 2009 was watched by a record Ligue 1 crowd of **78,056**. It was played at the Stade de France.

| 1956–57 | 1963–64 | 1966–67 | 1967–68 | 1968–69 | 1969–70 | 1973–74 | 1974–75 | 1975–76 | 1980–81 | 1985–86 |

Montpellier had a terrible disciplinary record in 2013-14, picking up **15 RED CARDS** in Ligue 1 – including **6** in the first **9 GAMES**!

In his first **3 LIGUE 1 GAMES** for Nice in 2016, 'Super' Mario Balotelli scored **5 GOALS**... and got **1 RED CARD**.

x12

Up to 2016 Marseille had been Ligue 1 runners-up a hefty **12 TIMES**, which is more than any other club in France.

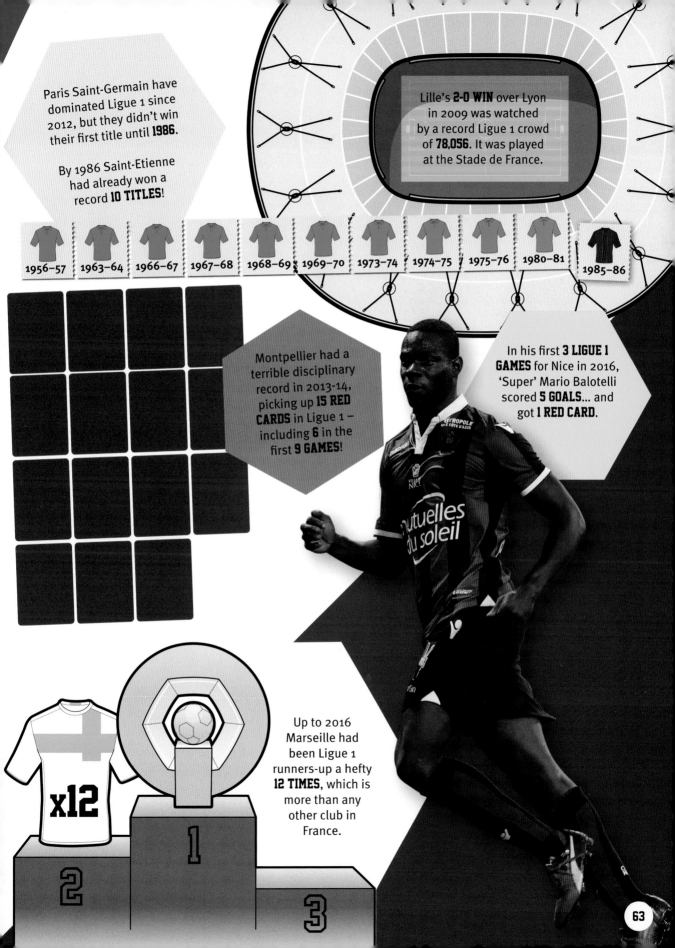

EUROPEAN LEAGUES: TEAMS

These European top-flight teams have bags of brain-busting numbers, facts and stats to reveal about their history and achievements.

ARIS ● **PAOK**

AE LARISSA ○

OLYMPIACOS ● ○ **AEK ATHENS**
PANATHINAIKOS

In 2006 Sporting Lisbon celebrated their **100TH ANNIVERSARY.** They released their **6TH CLUB BADGE,** which have all included the famous lion symbol.

Since the Greek championship was established in 1927 only **6 CLUBS** have won it. They are Olympiacos, Panathinaikos, AEK Athens, PAOK, Aris and AE Larissa.

N

Tromso, in Norway, is the northernmost professional club in Europe. But they have won **0 LEAGUE TITLES** since reaching the top flight in 1985.

The ground of Austrian clubs Sturm Graz and Grazer AK was called the Arnold Schwarzenegger Stadium for **8 YEARS**, named after the world-famous actor and body builder who was born near Graz.

UEFA NO TO RA

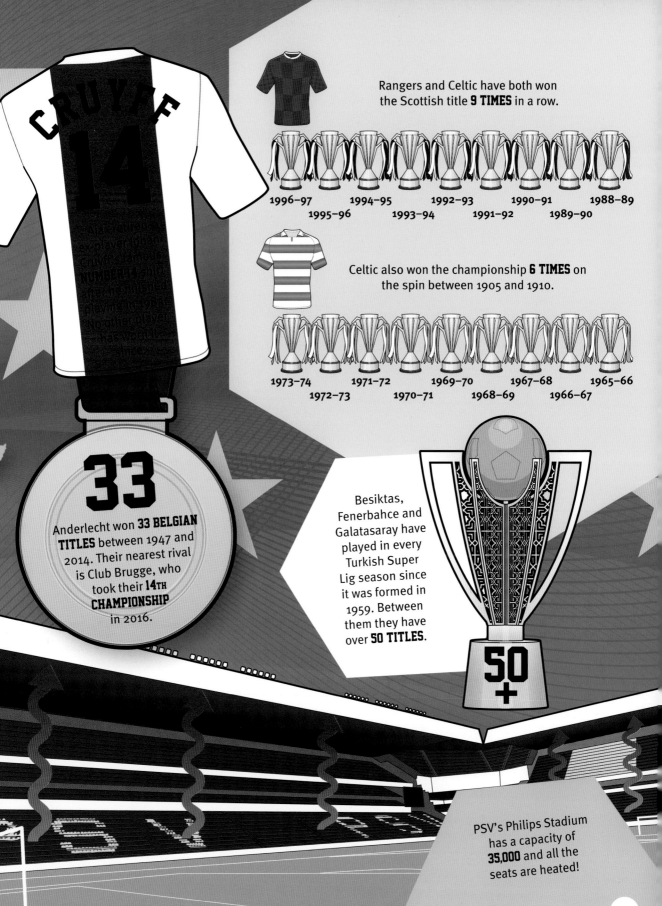

CRUYFF 14

Rangers and Celtic have both won the Scottish title **9 TIMES** in a row.

1996–97   1994–95   1992–93   1990–91   1988–89
1995–96   1993–94   1991–92   1989–90

Celtic also won the championship **6 TIMES** on the spin between 1905 and 1910.

1973–74   1971–72   1969–70   1967–68   1965–66
1972–73   1970–71   1968–69   1966–67

33

Anderlecht won **33 BELGIAN TITLES** between 1947 and 2014. Their nearest rival is Club Brugge, who took their **14TH CHAMPIONSHIP** in 2016.

Besiktas, Fenerbahce and Galatasaray have played in every Turkish Super Lig season since it was formed in 1959. Between them they have over **50 TITLES**.

50+

PSV's Philips Stadium has a capacity of **35,000** and all the seats are heated!

EUROPEAN LEAGUES: TEAMS 2

We're not done with our round-up of action across Europe just yet! Here, we jet set through countries like Bulgaria, Belarus, Serbia, Denmark and Poland.

 EURO '16

36 PLAYERS from Turkey's Super Lig were named in squads at EURO 2016. Surprisingly only **34 PLAYERS** from Spain's La Liga were.

16

Midfielder Scott Robinson is the youngest Scottish Premier League player. He was **16 YEARS, 1 MONTH AND 14 DAYS OLD** when he made his debut for Hearts in 2008.

Polish club Lech Poznan are known for a strange celebration, where fans turn their backs to the pitch and link arms. Manchester City copied it in **2010** and call it the 'Poznan'.

27

Red Star Belgrade claimed their **27TH LEAGUE TITLE** in 2016. It was also their **3RD TRIUMPH** since Serbia became independent in 2006.

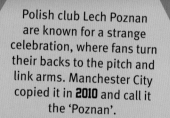

360:00

8 **14**

Belarus club BATE Borisov have played Barcelona in **4 CHAMPIONS LEAGUE GAMES**. They conceded **14 GOALS** and scored **0 GOALS**.

FC Copenhagen were only formed in 1992 but won their **11TH DANISH LEAGUE** in 2016.

Copenhagen's Parken Stadium also opened in 1992. It took **6 YEARS** before a hat-trick was scored there, by striker David Nielsen.

Dutch giants Ajax won all **3 MAJOR EUROPEAN TROPHIES** between 1987 and 1995. They lifted the Champions League, UEFA Cup and European Cup Winners' Cup.

26

Between 1933 and 2016 Levski Sofia were champions of Bulgaria a record **26 TIMES**. They also won **26 BULGARIA CUPS** in that time.

BAROS 12

Milan Baros joined Czech Republic club Banik Ostrava when he was **12 YEARS OLD**. He agreed to join Liverpool in 2001, but moved back to Banik **12 YEARS LATER**.

MAJOR LEAGUE SOCCER

MLS began in 1996 and 20 teams battle each season to win the MLS Cup. Time to take a trip to the States for these awesome American soccer stats!

NUMBER CRUNCH
DC United legend Jaime Moreno netted a record **44 PENALTIES** from **52 ATTEMPTS.**

DC United, Houston Dynamo and LA Galaxy have all won the MLS Cup **3 YEARS IN A ROW.**

37,260
Keeper Kevin Hartman played a huge **416 GAMES** and appeared for a record-breaking **37,260 MINUTES** in the MLS between 1997 and 2013.

Most MLS Cup victories

Team		Years
LA Galaxy	5	2014, 2012, 2011, 2005, 2002
DC United	4	2004, 1999, 1997, 1996
San Jose Earthquakes	2	2003, 2001
Houston Dynamo	2	2007, 2006
Columbus Crew SC	1	2008
Chicago Fire	1	1998
Portland Timbers	1	2015
Colorado Rapids	1	2010
Real Salt Lake	1	2009

In his first **4 REGULAR SEASONS** with New York Red Bulls, Bradley Wright-Phillips belted **98 GOALS** in just **107 GAMES**. He won his **2ND MLS GOLDEN BOOT** in 2016.

In **406 MLS GAMES**, Kyle Beckerman made a record **614 FOULS**. He also received **93 YELLOW CARDS** and **4 RED**.

The Supporters' Shield is won by the team with most points in the regular season. LA Galaxy and DC United both have **4 VICTORIES**.

Landon Donovan is the MLS all-time top scorer. He struck **145 GOALS** in **340 GAMES** for LA Galaxy and San Jose Earthquakes.

Donovan also has **136 ASSISTS** in the league.

David Beckham won **2 MLS CUPS** with LA Galaxy. In **98 REGULAR-SEASON GAMES** he clocked up **40 ASSISTS**.

CRAZY CLUB FACTS

Football isn't just about the glitz, the glamour, the goals and the glory – sometimes the strange and silly stuff is just as incredible!

Fans of Bayern Munich and TSV 1860 Munich consumed **700,000 SAUSAGES** at the Allianz Arena in season 2005-06.

11-1

Real Madrid once beat their biggest rivals, Barcelona, by an astonishing score of **11-1** in a cup game in 1943.

Leicester City spent **140 DAYS** at the bottom of the Premier League in 2014-15, but still avoided relegation. The following season they won the title!

On 23 December 2009 Barcelona won their **6TH TROPHY OF THE YEAR**. They lifted La Liga, UEFA Champions League, UEFA Super Cup, Spanish Super Cup, Copa del Ray and Club World Cup – happy Christmas, boys!

74

MANCHESTER UNITED

WEST BROMWICH ALBION

98:00

5

5

Sir Alex Ferguson's final game as Manchester United manager was a crazy **5-5 DRAW** with West Bromwich Albion. That's the highest-scoring draw in the Premier League.

BECKAM 7

Despite winning **6 PREMIER LEAGUE TITLES** and being one of the most famous players in the world, David Beckham once had the name on his shirt spelt wrong!

Juventus are the only club to have won all **5 UEFA COMPETITIONS** – the Champions League, UEFA Cup, Cup Winners' Cup, Super Cup and Intercontinental Cup.

NUMBER CRUNCH
In 2012 Sevilla remodelled their subs' bench as a **10-METRE LONG HOTDOG** as part of a sponsorship deal!

QPR began the 2012-13 season without winning any of their first **16 PREMIER LEAGUE GAMES**.

LLLLLL
LLLLLLLLLL

WORLD CUP

This section of *Football Number Crunch* cranks out all the numbers and stats connected to international football, starting with the World Cup.

Brazil are the only team to have played in every World Cup finals tournament – that's **20 TOURNAMENTS** in total.

Germany (**106 GAMES**) and Brazil (**104**) are the only **2 COUNTRIES** to have played over **100 GAMES** at the World Cup.

NUMBER CRUNCH
England's **1st WORLD CUP FINALS GAME** was in 1950. They beat Chile **2-0** in Brazil.

They've only played **77 WORLD CUP GAMES**, but Argentina have received a record **120 CARDS**. That's **111 YELLOWS**, **8 STRAIGHT REDS** and **1 DOUBLE YELLOW** resulting in red.

The 2010 World Cup final between Spain and the Netherlands saw an incredible **14 YELLOW CARDS** and **1 RED CARD** dished out.

World Cup finals 1930–2014...

1930
Uruguay 4-2 Argentina

1934
Italy 2-1 Czechoslovakia

1938
Italy 4-2 Hungary

1950
Uruguay 2-1 Brazil*

1954
West Germany 3-2 Hungary

1958
Brazil 5-2 Sweden

1962
Brazil 3-1 Czechoslovakia

1966
England 4-2 West Germany

1970
Brazil 4-1 Italy

1974
West Germany 2-1 Netherlands

1978
Argentina 3-1 Netherlands

1982
Italy 3-1 West Germany

1986
Argentina 3-2 West Germany

1990
West Germany 1-0 Argentina

1994
Brazil 0-0 Italy
Brazil won 3-2 on penalties

1998
France 3-0 Brazil

2002
Brazil 2-0 Germany

2006
Italy 1-1 France
Italy won 5-3 on penalties

2010
Spain 1-0 Netherlands

2014
Germany 1-0 Argentina

*Deciding match of a four-team final group, which is the only time a World Cup has not been decided by a one-match final.

A record **171 GOALS** were scored at the 1998 and 2014 World Cups.

171
1998, 2014

The lowest-scoring World Cups were in 1930 and 1934, when **70 GOALS** were scored.

70
1930, 1934

Germany have appeared in **18 WORLD CUP TOURNAMENTS.** Only once, in 1934, did they fail to reach the quarter-finals.

The highest attendance was in 1954, when **173,850 FANS** watched Uruguay beat Brazil 2-1 at the Maracana stadium in Rio.

173,850

1954

AUSTRIA

7

SWITZERLAND

5

A record **12 GOALS** were scored in one World Cup finals match in 1954, when Austria beat Switzerland **7-5.**

Germany have had **4 PENALTY SHOOTOUTS** at World Cup tournaments, winning all of them.

England have been involved in **3 PENALTY SHOOTOUTS,** losing every single one.

WORLD CUP 2

Let's look at the World Cup stars and heroes who have set records on the biggest international football stage.

NUMBER CRUNCH
Diego Maradona captained Argentina in a record **16 WORLD CUP GAMES**. He also scored **8 GOALS**, and received **4 YELLOW CARDS** and **1 RED CARD**.

Russia's Oleg Salenko scored a record **5 GOALS IN ONE GAME** against Cameroon at the 1994 tournament.

The oldest player at a World Cup was Faryd Mondragon. He was **43 YEARS AND 3 DAYS OLD** when he played in goal for Colombia in 2014.

Northern Ireland midfielder Norman Whiteside is the youngest player at the finals. He was **17 YEARS AND 41 DAYS OLD** at the 1982 finals.

25

Germany midfielder Lothar Matthäus played in a record **25 WORLD CUP GAMES** between 1982 and 1998. He won the competition as captain in 1990.

Right-back Cafu played in **3 WORLD CUP FINALS IN A ROW** in 1994, 1998 and 2002. He was Brazil's captain as they won the trophy in 2002.

Brazil striker Pelé is the only player to win **3 WORLD CUP WINNER'S MEDALS**. He was a champion in 1958, 1962 and 1970.

1958 **1962** **1970**

Italy goalkeeper Gianluigi Buffon has played in a record-equaling **5 WORLD CUP TOURNAMENTS** (1998-2014).

He shares the record with Mexican keeper Antonio Carbajal (1950-66) and Germany's Lothar Matthäus (1982-98).

BUFFON

Germany forward Thomas Müller ran an incredible **83,957 METRES** at the 2014 World Cup. That's the same as running an Olympic athletics track **210 TIMES**!

Top goalscorers at World Cup tournaments

Player		Tournaments
Miroslav Klose		2014, 2010, 2006, 2002
Ronaldo		2006, 2002, 1998, 1994
Gerd Müller		1974, 1970
Just Fontaine		1958
Pelé		1970, 1966, 1962, 1958
Sandor Kocsis		1954
Jürgen Klinsmann		1998, 1994, 1990
Helmut Rahn		1958, 1954
Gary Lineker		1990, 1986
Gabriel Batistuta		2002, 1998, 1994
Teofilo Cubillas		1982, 1978, 1970
Thomas Müller		2014, 2010
Grzegorz Lato		1982, 1978, 1974

WORLD CUP 3

From the first goal to the fastest sending off, here are even more fascinating facts and numbers from World Cup tournaments.

HUNGARY		EL SALVADOR
10	90:00	1

Laszlo Kiss scored the fastest World Cup hat-trick. The Hungary striker netted **3** in just **8 MINUTES** in a **10-1 WIN** over El Salvador in 1982.

Kiss was also a substitute and didn't come on until the **56TH MINUTE**.

France's **4-1 WIN** over Mexico was the **1ST EVER WORLD CUP GAME**, in 1930. Frenchman Lucien Laurent scored the **1ST GOAL**.

Italy keeper Walter Zenga kept **5 CLEAN SHEETS IN A ROW** at the 1990 World Cup. He didn't concede a goal for **517 MINUTES**.

Italy	1-0	Austria
Italy	1-0	USA
Italy	2-0	Czechoslovakia
Italy	2-0	Uruguay
Italy	1-0	Rep. of Ireland

Coach Luiz Felipe Scolari went **12 WORLD CUP GAMES** without defeat – **7** with Brazil in 2002 and **5** with Portugal in 2006.

Only **2 PLAYERS** have been sent off **TWICE** in the World Cup – France's Zinedine Zidane in 1998 and 2006, and Cameroon's Rigobert Song in 1994 and '98.

When Spain were World Cup winners in 2010, only **3 PLAYERS** scored for them – David Villa, Andres Iniesta (*right*) and Carles Puyol.

Miroslav Klose's first World Cup goal was on 1 June 2002, his last on 8 July 2014. That's an amazing **12 YEARS, 1 MONTH AND 7 DAYS** between the first and last.

00:52

The fastest red card at the World Cup was after just **52 SECONDS**. Uruguay's José Batista was sent off for a bad tackle against Scotland in 1986.

ORDEM E PROGRESSO

WOMEN'S WORLD CUP

Since the first competition in 1991, the Women's World Cup has grown rapidly to become a hugely popular international event. Check out these facts and numbers...

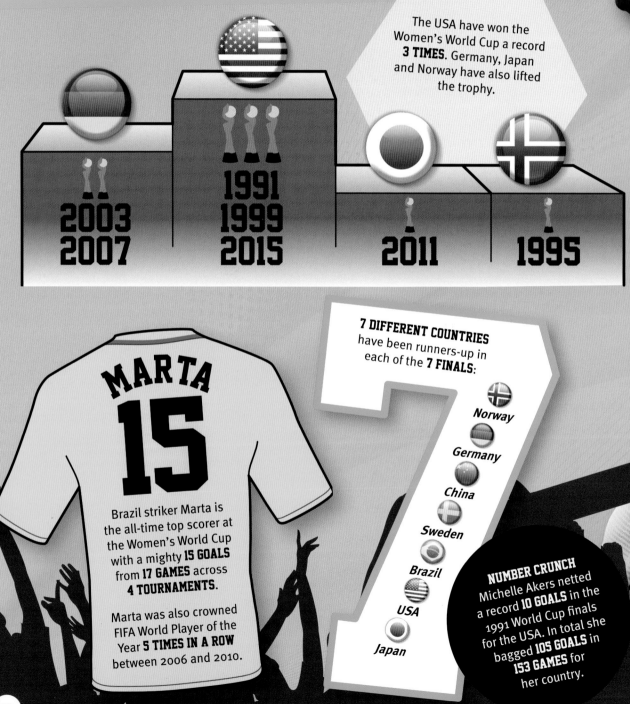

The USA have won the Women's World Cup a record **3 TIMES**. Germany, Japan and Norway have also lifted the trophy.

2003 2007

1991 1999 2015

2011

1995

MARTA
15

Brazil striker Marta is the all-time top scorer at the Women's World Cup with a mighty **15 GOALS** from **17 GAMES** across **4 TOURNAMENTS**.

Marta was also crowned FIFA World Player of the Year **5 TIMES IN A ROW** between 2006 and 2010.

7 DIFFERENT COUNTRIES have been runners-up in each of the **7 FINALS**:

Norway

Germany

China

Sweden

Brazil

USA

Japan

NUMBER CRUNCH
Michelle Akers netted a record **10 GOALS** in the 1991 World Cup finals for the USA. In total she bagged **105 GOALS** in **153 GAMES** for her country.

90:00

Germany and Argentina are big World Cup rivals. In 2007 the German women's team thrashed Argentina by a record score of **11-0**.

11

0

BEHRINGER 12', 24'
GAREFREKES 17'
PRINZ 29', 45+1', 59'
LINGOR 51', 90+1'
SMISEK 57', 70', 79'

Carli Lloyd scored the **1st WOMEN'S WORLD CUP FINAL HAT-TRICK** when the USA beat Japan 5-2 in 2015. All her goals came in the first **16 MINUTES**.

The USA have scored a record **112 GOALS** at the finals.

146
2015

A record **146 GOALS** were scored at the 2015 Women's World Cup.

Just **86** were netted in 2011.

86
2011

90,185

NUMBER CRUNCH
At the most recent World Cup in 2015, **24 COUNTRIES** competed – that's double the number that took part in the first in 1991.

83

EUROPEAN CHAMPIONSHIP

The most prestigious international trophy in Europe is the UEFA European Championship. It began in 1960, and Portugal took the title at EURO 2016.

Germany and Spain have both won the EUROs a record **3 TIMES**.

Since 1972, Germany have only failed to finish in the top **TOP 4** at **1 TOURNAMENT**.

Spain became the first country to win the trophy **2 TIMES IN A ROW**, in 2008 and 2012.

France is the only country to have hosted the EUROs **3 TIMES**.

The Henri Delaunay cup, which is the trophy the winners receive, is **60CM TALL** and weighs **8KG**.

NUMBER CRUNCH
2,427,303
That's the number of fans who attended games at the EURO 2016 finals in France.

Check out every final between 1960 and 2016...

1960
Soviet Union 2-1 Yugoslavia

1964
Spain 2-1 Soviet Union

1968
Italy 2-0 Yugoslavia

1972
West Germany 3-0 Soviet Union

1976
Czechoslovakia 2-2 West Germany
Czechoslovakia won 5-3 on penalties

1980
West Germany 2-1 Belgium

1984
France 2-0 Spain

1988
Netherlands 2-0 Soviet Union

1992
Denmark 2-0 Germany

1996
Germany 2-1 Czech Republic

2000
France 2-1 Italy

2004
Greece 1-0 Portugal

2008
Spain 1-0 Germany

2012
Spain 4-0 Italy

2016
Portugal 1-0 France

+72

Germany have scored the most European Championship goals **(72)** but also conceded the most **(48)**.

-48

1972 **1996**

Berti Vogts has **2 EURO WINNER'S MEDALS** – 1 as a squad player with West Germany in 1972 and 1 as Germany's manager in 1996.

EURO 2016 finalists Portugal and France both had **121 ATTEMPTS** at goal during the tournament. France hit the woodwork a record **6 TIMES**.

The winners Portugal (*below*) won only **1** of their **7 GAMES** in normal time. They drew their first **3 GAMES**.

Norway have only played in **1 TOURNAMENT**, at EURO 2000. They won **1 GAME**, lost 1 and drew 1, scoring **1 GOAL** and conceding **1 GOAL**.

EDER

RAFA

EUROPEAN CHAMPIONSHIP 2

Ronaldo, Platini, Müller, Griezmann, Sanches, Bierhoff – these pages are crammed with cool facts about the biggest Euro Championship players.

Renato Sanches was just **18 YEARS AND 328 DAYS OLD** when he won EURO 2016 with Portugal. He's the youngest EUROs winner.

Hungary keeper Gabor Kiraly (*left*) also set a record in 2016 as the oldest player at the finals. He was **40 YEARS AND 86 DAYS OLD**.

3 GERMAN PLAYERS have scored **2 GOALS** in a EURO final – Gerd Müller, Horst Hrubesch and Oliver Bierhoff.

Bierhoff scored the **1st GOLDEN GOAL** at the EUROs when he bagged a **95TH MINUTE** sudden death winner against the Czech Republic in 1996.

NUMBER CRUNCH
France's Antoine Griezmann top-scored at EURO 2016 with **6 GOALS**. Behind him were 6 **PLAYERS**, all with **3 GOALS**.

Spain midfielder Cesc Fabregas scored winning penalties in shootouts at **2 TOURNAMENTS** – EURO 2008 and EURO 2012.

Michel Platini scored a record **2 HAT-TRICKS** for France at the 1984 tournament.

The fastest goal at a EURO was after **67 SECONDS**. Dmitri Kirichenko scored it for Russia against Greece at EURO 2004.

Robert Lewandowski hit the net just **100 SECONDS** into Poland's EURO 2016 quarter-final with Portugal.

Spain keeper Iker Casillas was named in a record **5 EUROPEAN CHAMPIONSHIP SQUADS** between 2000 and 2016.

France speedster Kingsley Coman was the fastest player at EURO 2016. He hit a top speed of **32.8 KILOMETRES PER HOUR.**

Cristiano Ronaldo had a record-breaking EURO 2016...

- Most appearances at European Championships – **21 GAMES.**
- Joint-highest European Championship scorer – **9 GOALS.**
- First player to score at **4 EUROPEAN CHAMPIONSHIPS.**
- Played a record **128TH PORTUGAL GAME.**
- Reached **29 GOALS** in EURO qualifying and finals tournaments.

Top EURO finals goalscorers of all time...

9 goals	Cristiano Ronaldo	(Portugal)
9 goals	Michel Platini	(France)
7 goals	Alan Shearer	(England)
6 goals	Antoine Griezmann	(France)
6 goals	Zlatan Ibrahimovic	(Sweden)
6 goals	Thierry Henry	(France)

COPA AMERICA

South American footy fans go crazy for the Copa America, the most famous international competition on the continent.

The Copa America began in 1916 – here are all the countries that have won it...

Uruguay	15 titles
Argentina	14 titles
Brazil	8 titles
Chile	2 titles
Peru	2 titles
Paraguay	2 titles
Colombia	1 title
Bolivia	1 title

Argentina have been Copa America runners-up a record **14 TIMES**.

Brazil had to wait **40 YEARS** between winning their third title in 1949 and their fourth in 1989.

Chile won their **1st COPA AMERICA** in 2015 and their **2nd** the following year.

Lionel Messi has never won the Copa America. He's been a losing finalist **3 TIMES** – in 2007, 2015 and 2016.

Messi became Argentina's record scorer at Copa America 2016, hitting his **55th INTERNATIONAL GOAL**.

Messi scored a hat-trick in just **19 MINUTES** against Panama at the 2016 tournament.

Brazil hero Zizinho and Argentina's Norberto Mendez are Copa America's top scorers, with **17 GOALS**.

Japan played **3 GAMES** at the 1999 Copa America, even though it's an Asian country!

In **2016** Arsenal's Alexis Sanchez won the Golden Ball as best player. Manchester City keeper Claudio Bravo won the keeper's Golden Glove award.

Uruguay star Luis Suárez won his first Copa America in 2011. He scored **4 GOALS** and was named Most Valuable Player.

GOLD CUP

This is the competition to discover the best country in North America, Central America and the Caribbean. Now you can discover this bunch of fab facts about it...

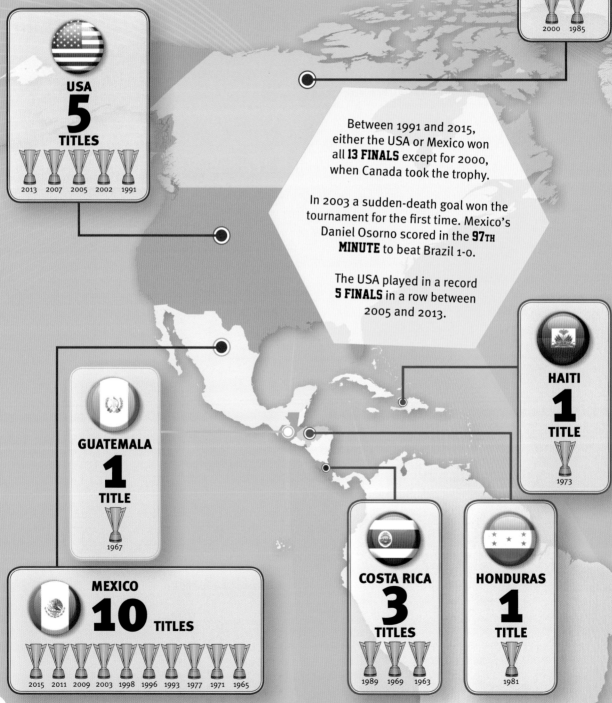

CANADA
2
TITLES
2000 1985

USA
5
TITLES
2013 2007 2005 2002 1991

Between 1991 and 2015, either the USA or Mexico won all **13 FINALS** except for 2000, when Canada took the trophy.

In 2003 a sudden-death goal won the tournament for the first time. Mexico's Daniel Osorno scored in the **97TH MINUTE** to beat Brazil 1-0.

The USA played in a record **5 FINALS** in a row between 2005 and 2013.

HAITI
1
TITLE
1973

GUATEMALA
1
TITLE
1967

MEXICO
10 TITLES
2015 2011 2009 2003 1998 1996 1993 1977 1971 1965

COSTA RICA
3
TITLES
1989 1969 1963

HONDURAS
1
TITLE
1981

Brazil have played **14 GOLD CUP GAMES** after being invited to play in the event. They were runners-up in 1996 and 2003.

From 2002, USA hero Landon Donovan scored a record **18 GOLD CUP GOALS** across **6 DIFFERENT TOURNAMENTS.**

The 2015 Gold Cup was held in **2 COUNTRIES,** the USA and Canada.

Ex-Real Madrid and Manchester United striker Javier Hernandez top-scored with **7 GOALS** when Mexico won the Gold Cup in 2011. Another Mexican, Luis Roberto Alves, hit a record **11 GOALS** at the 1993 Gold Cup.

AFRICA CUP OF NATIONS

Held every two years, the Africa Cup of Nations features awesome countries such as Ghana, Cameroon and Ivory Coast. Find out all about its top stars and teams.

EGYPT
7 TITLES
2010 2008 2006 1998 1986 1959 1957

Just **3 COUNTRIES** – Egypt, Sudan and Ethiopia – contested the first tournament in 1957.

GHANA
4 TITLES
1982 1978 1965 1963

IVORY COAST
2 TITLES
2015 1992

NIGERIA
3 TITLES
2013 1994 1980

Guinea-Bissau reached the 2017 finals for the first time after beating Zambia 3-2 in qualifying. In that game they scored a dramatic **97TH-MINUTE** winner.

Egyptian striker Ad-Diba scored a record **4 GOALS** in the 1957 Africa Cup of Nations final.

CAMEROON
5 TITLES
2017 2002 2000 1988 1984

DR CONGO
2 TITLES
1974 1968

1 TITLE

| Zambia 2012 | Tunisia 2004 | Sudan 1970 | Algeria 1990 |
| Ethiopia 1962 | Morocco 1976 | South Africa 1996 | Congo 1972 |

Every player on the pitch took a penalty in the 1992 final. Ivory Coast eventually beat Ghana **11-10** on penalties – **24 PENS** were taken in the shootout!

Ghana have lost in the final a record **5 TIMES** – in 1968, 1970, 1992, 2010 and 2015.

Famous Cameroon striker Samuel Eto'o smashed in a record **18 TOURNAMENT GOALS** in total. He was top scorer in 2006 and 2008.

Ghana coach Charles Gyamfi and Egypt's Hassan Shehata are the only managers to win the tournament on **3 OCCASIONS.**

A record **99 GOALS** were scored at the 2008 Africa Cup of Nations.

Just 7 were scored in 1957, but only **2 GAMES** were played that year.

99 2008

7 1957

93

INTERNATIONAL LEGENDS

Here are some of the finest footballers ever to grace the international game, plus a collection of super stats all about them.

PELE

Superstar Pelé scored an unbelievable **1,281 GOALS** in **1,363 GAMES** in all competitions. He played for Brazil in the 1950s, '60s and '70s.

NUMBER CRUNCH
Miroslav Klose is Germany's all-time top scorer with **71 GOALS** in **137 GAMES**, but Gerd Müller blasted a staggering **68 GOALS** in just **62 GAMES**!

Abby Wambach holds the record for scoring the most international goals. She notched **184 GOALS** for the USA between 2001 and 2015.

The Netherlands' Johan Cruyff is regarded as the best European player ever. He won **3 EUROPEAN CUPS** with Ajax and **3 EUROPEAN FOOTBALLER OF THE YEAR AWARDS**.

Brazil captain Neymar is mega prolific in official FIFA games, scoring **20** in his first **34 GAMES.** Overall, he has scored an incredible **50 GOALS** in **74 GAMES** for Brazil.

Lionel Messi was crowned World Player of the Year **5 TIMES** between 2009 and 2015.

Argentina ace Diego Maradona scored the best World Cup goal ever in 1986, against England. He took the ball in his own half, then beat **4 PLAYERS** and the keeper in just **11 SECONDS** to bag a brilliant solo strike.

NUMBER CRUNCH
Cristiano Ronaldo has scored a modest **3 GOALS** in **13 WORLD CUP FINALS GAMES,** but as of February 2017 he had netted a huge **22** in **32 WORLD CUP QUALIFIERS.**

INIESTA
6
Andres Iniesta has won **1 WORLD CUP** and **2 EUROs** with Spain. The magical midfielder is the only player to win **6 UEFA MAN OF THE MATCH** awards at the EUROs.

France's Fabien Barthez and England's Peter Shilton kept a record **10 CLEAN SHEETS** in World Cup finals games.

US keeper Hope Solo kept a record **100TH INTERNATIONAL CLEAN SHEET** in July 2016.

PICTURE CREDITS

The publishers would like to thank the following sources for their kind permission to reproduce the pictures in this book. The page numbers for each of the photographs are listed below, giving the page on which they appear in the book and any location indicator (T = top, B = bottom C = centre, L = left, R = right).

FreeVectorMaps.com: 9L, 30R, 54, 58, 64TR, 66-67, 90, 92

Getty Images: /Allsport: 24; /Matthew Ashton-AMA: 41; /Evrim Aydin/Anadolu Agency: 20R; /Lars Baron/Bongarts: 14; /Robyn Beck/AFP: 73BR; /Al Bello: 94; /Alex Caparros: 19R, 21, 56; /Jean Catuffe: 87; /Fabrice Coffrini/AFP: 77; /Franck Crusiaux/Gamma-Rapho: 62BR; /Patricia de Melo Moreira/AFP: 64B; /Denis Doyle: 57; /Stephen Dunn: 72-73B; /Paul Ellis/AFP: 69L; /Franck Fife/AFP: 28; /fotopress: 23; /Stuart Franklin: 83; /Chris Furlong: 31R; /GASPA/ullstein bild: 17; /Lluis Gene/AFP: 71B; /Laurence Griffiths: 86BR; /Valery Hache/AFP: 63; /Matthias Hangst/Bongarts: 34, 53C; /Ronny Hartmann/Bongarts: 16; /A. Hassenstein/FC Bayern: 13; /Mike Hewitt: 71R, 85; /Stan Honda/AFP: 91L; /Jose Jordan/AFP: 19L; /Jasper Juinen: 81C; /Gerard Julien/AFP: 69R; /Nicholas Kamm/AFP: 88; /Mike Kireev/Epsilon: 31L; /Kirill Kudryavtsev/AFP: 37BR; /Maurizio Lagana: 27; /Christian Liewig/Corbis: 62L; /Alex Livesey: 11R, 42; /Juan Mabromata/AFP: 95; /Jamie McDonald: 43, 59; /Dean Mouhtaropoulos: 7; /Metin Pala/Anadolu Agency: 86L; /Valerio Pennicino: 60; /Power Sport Images: 39T; /Lennart Preiss/Bongarts: 1, 51; /David Price/Arsenal FC: 8; /Federico Proietti/Anadolu Agency: 25TL; /Tom Purslow/Manchester United FC: 10; /Manuel Queimadelos Alonso: 22; /Wojtek Radwanski/EuroFootball: 66; /Michael Regan: 46, 74; /Lars Ronbog/FrontZoneSport: 67; /Martin Rose: 29; /sampics/Corbis: 15; /Issouf Sanogo /AFP: 93; /Alexandre Simoes/Borussia Dortmund: 12; /Wally Skalij/Los Angeles Times: 91BR; /Patrik Stollarz/AFP: 37L; /Bob Thomas: 80; /Bob Thomas/Popperfoto: 79; /Pedro Ugarte/AFP: 81L; /VI-Images: 40; /Claudio Villa: 53B; /Darren Walsh/Chelsea FC: 11BL, 49; /Ian Walton: 6; /Andrew Yates/AFP: 47

PA Images: /Matthew Ashton/Empics: 33; /Tony Marshall/Empics: 30L

Shutterstock: /AGIF: 38L, 38RT; /CP DC Press: 39BL; /imagestockdesign: 39BR; /Herbert Kratky: 38TR; /Andrey Kuzmin: 25BR, 30R, 81R; /LevateMedia: 38RB; /Maxisport: 38BR, 39TL; /mr3002: 39L; /Natursports: 39R; /Ninell: 36; /Cornelia Viljoen: 20L; /Marcos Mesa Sam Wordley: 39TR

Every effort has been made to acknowledge correctly and contact the source and/or copyright holder of each picture and Carlton Books Limited apologises for any unintentional errors or omissions that will be corrected in future editions of this book.